A Practical Guide to Learning Disabilities

Denise Destrempes-Marquez and Louise Lafleur

D0994705

Éditions de l'Hôpital Sainte-Justine

Mother and Child University Hospital Centre

Canadian Cataloguing in Publication Data

Destrempes-Marquez, Denise

A practical guide to learning disabilities

(Parenting)
Translation of: Les troubles d'apprentissage: comprendre et intervenir
Includes bibliographical references.

ISBN 2-921858-92-4

1. Learning disabilities. I. Lafleur, Louise Bastien. II. Hôpital Sainte-Justine. III. Title. IV. Series: Parenting (Montreal, Quebec).

RJ496.L4D4713 2001   618.92'85889   C00-942107-6

Translation: Elaine Kennedy and Marcia Barr

Cover illustration: Prétexte Communication Graphique

Cover design and computer graphics: Céline Forget

Publications Service, Hôpital Sainte-Justine
3175, chemin de la Côte-Sainte-Catherine
Montreal, Quebec H3T 1C5
Telephone: (514) 345-4671
Fax: (514) 345-4631

Legal deposit: Bibliothèque nationale du Québec, 1999

ACKNOWLEDGMENTS

▼

This book embodies the results of more than 30 years of unflagging work by a large number of volunteers with the Learning Disabilities Association of Canada (LDAC) and the Learning Disabilities Association of Quebec (LDAQ). We would like to express our sincere thanks to them as well as to the specialists and friends of LDAQ who have generously allowed us to use excerpts from their publications.

We would also like to thank Lorraine Diotte and Gail Desnoyers for their valuable comments, Christine Couston and Suzanne Lavoie for their technical assistance and enthusiasm, and Luc Begin, our editor and publisher, for his support throughout the preparation of this book.

Table of Contents
▼

INTRODUCTION

▼

Many parents have a child struggling with difficulties in school and problems interacting with others. This book is intended for them; it is designed to provide them with the support they need to help their son or daughter as effectively as possible from the time he or she starts school through to the adolescent years. While parents may suspect their preschooler is experiencing problems, it is generally not until children start school that their learning disabilities become apparent. And at that point, parents, often very concerned, start to seek advice and support.

Intended as a practical guide, this book starts out by defining learning disabilities and emphasizing the fact that they are not due to a lack of intelligence, but rather to difficulties acquiring and processing information. It goes on to describe some of the most common learning disabilities—dyslexia, auditory processing deficit, language disorders and attention deficit disorders—on the basis of information obtained, in part, from well-known official organizations and associations in the field. It then addresses such practical issues as the evaluation of learning disabilities and the services available through the school. The final chapters offer answers to some of the questions most frequently asked by parents, list readily accessible resources, and provide checklists for detecting early warning signs of learning disabilities.

The objective of this guide is two-fold: to help parents understand the difficulties their child is experiencing, and to enable them to take effective action in assisting their child and in dealing with the different professionals involved. It seeks to achieve this objective by presenting basic information on learning disabilities and their manifestations and by suggesting practical means of approach. This project has grown out of our experience as parents and our long-term involvement with the Learning Disabilities Association of Quebec.

We have chosen to use the term *learning disabilities* because it is the expression generally used in North America to describe all learning-related disorders, including dyslexia. It should be noted, however, that *dyslexia* is the term most commonly used in Europe to refer to these disorders.

We hope readers will come away with the conviction that people with learning disabilities can lead full, happy and fulfilling lives. Well-informed parents who are determined to help their child can contribute more than anyone to their child's success, because their attitudes and courses of action will have a decisive influence.

CHAPTER 1

UNDERSTANDING LEARNING DISABILITIES

▼

Early Warning Signs

Parents are generally the first to notice that their child behaves or learns differently from other children the same age. However, the initial signs of a learning disability can be difficult to detect; sometimes a disability does not become apparent until the child is exposed to complex tasks at school.

Before a child begins school, the parents may notice that he or she is late starting to talk or has difficulty pronouncing common words or following instructions. The child might find it difficult to engage in play activities, either alone or with other children. The child might be easily confused when performing tasks such as getting dressed or tying his or her shoelaces. While these are not necessarily signs of a learning disability, they should not be ignored.

There are a number of signs that can indicate a learning disability including excessive crying, an inordinate amount of anxiety about changes in routine, difficulty learning to jump or to bounce a ball, problems eating and sleeping, impulsive behaviour causing self-inflicted injury or harm to friends, a tendency to be gloomy or agitated between activities, an inability to sense danger, and great difficulty learning songs and nursery rhymes. Appendix 1, "Checklists for Detecting Early Warning Signs of Learning Disabilities", provides more detailed information on these signs.

To sum up, learning disabilities are not always obvious. However, there are indications that can alert parents to the problem and prompt them to take action as early as possible.

Stages in the Learning Process

Learning is the process of acquiring knowledge and skills. It includes a number of stages. First, information is recorded in the brain; this is the *input* or *perception* stage. Then, it must be organized and understood — the *integration* or *decoding* stage. Once recorded and understood, information must be stored for later retrieval — the *retention* or *memory* stage. Finally, it must be communicated from the brain to the outside world or be reflected in action — the *production* or *output* stage. Learning disabilities can occur in any of these four areas.[1]

Learning Difficulties and Learning Disabilities

There is a significant difference between learning difficulties and learning disabilities. Learning difficulties are temporary, periodic problems that prevent a child from learning. They are caused by factors external to the child — separation from parents, change of school, change of teaching methods, etc.— and are reflected in:

- problems concentrating (the child is distracted, moody)
- trouble reading, writing and doing arithmetic
- behaviour problems (the child is aggressive, sad).

---

1. This information is from a booklet for parents by Dr. Larry B. Silver entitled *ADHD: Attention Deficit-Hyperactivity Disorder and Learning Disabilities*, published by CIBA-GEIGY in 1989.

Learning disabilities are permanent, persistent problems. They are intrinsic to the child, but are not related to the child's intelligence. They affect the child's learning and behaviour and are the cause of repeated failures in school. Learning disabilities can have an impact on:

- attention span, memory and reasoning
- coordination, communication, and the ability to read and write
- conceptualization, sociability and emotional maturity.

With early detection and appropriate action, however, learning-challenged children can learn to live with their disabilities, compensate for them by drawing on their strengths, and improve their performance in areas of skill difficulty.

Brief Background and Terminology

As learning disabilities were recognized and studied, different terms were adopted to describe them. Prior to the 1940s, children who had difficulty learning or paying attention were considered mentally retarded, emotionally disturbed or culturally disadvantaged. The research of the 1940s identified a fourth group of children: those whose difficulties were neurologically based or due to the way their nervous systems worked. Initially this disorder was called *minimal brain damage*, and later *minimal brain dysfunction*. These terms were used to refer to children suffering from problems in school which were neurologically based: hyperactivity, short attention span, impulsivity and emotional problems. Today, the term *learning disability* is used to designate all learning-related disorders.[2]

---

2. Ibid.

What are Learning Disabilities?

The official definition of *learning disabilities*, adopted on October 18, 1981 by the Canadian Association for Children and Adults with Learning Disabilities, is as follows:

"*Learning disabilities* is a generic term that refers to a heterogeneous group of disorders due to identifiable or inferred central nervous system dysfunction. Such disorders may be manifested by delays in early development and/or difficulties in any of the following areas: attention, memory, reasoning, coordination, communicating, reading, writing, spelling, calculation, social competence and emotional maturation.

"Learning disabilities are intrinsic to the individual, and many affect learning and behaviour in any individual including those with potentially average, average or above average intelligence.

"Learning disabilities are not due primarily to visual, hearing or motor handicaps; to mental retardation, emotional disturbance or environmental disadvantage; although they may occur concurrently with any of these.

"Learning disabilities may arise from genetic variations, biochemical factors, events in the pre to peri-natal period, or any other subsequent events resulting in neurological impairment."

In 1988, the National Joint Committee on Learning Disabilities defined *learning disabilities* as "a general term that refers to a heterogeneous group of disorders manifested by significant difficulties in the acquisition and use of listening, speaking, reading, writing, reasoning, or mathematical abilities."

In Europe, the term *dyslexia* is often used in a general sense, encompassing both oral and written language disabilities. Dyslexia is discussed in detail in Chapter 2.

The terms *serious learning difficulties* and *specific learning difficulties*, as defined by the Quebec Department of Education, are discussed in Appendix 2.

Causes of Learning Disabilities

An estimated 10 to 15 percent of the population is affected by learning disabilities. This means, for example, that over 700,000 people in Quebec live with a handicap of this nature.

We have seen that learning disabilities are not due to a lack of intelligence, but rather to a disorder in the acquisition and processing of information. We know that learning disabilities can occur to varying degrees in children from the same family; researchers are currently striving to isolate the gene that may be responsible. Other factors causing learning disabilities may be related to events that occur during pregnancy, childbirth or infancy: exposure to certain drugs or other toxic products before or after birth, hormonal or immune system disorders, low birth weight or malnutrition, chemotherapy or radiation during the child's early years. A combination of these and other factors may contribute to the incidence of learning disabilities among children.

All parents are concerned about the health and well-being of their children and may blame themselves for the problems a child is experiencing. But research shows that learning disabilities are not due to poor parenting, parental absence from the home, a lack of reading or talking to the child, or developmental disorders.

People with learning disabilities have a hidden handicap and can thus blend in with the crowd. This is not necessarily a blessing, because it can make it harder for them to get the help they need.

Manifestations of Learning Disabilities [3]

Specialists often use technical or scientific terms to describe learning disabilities. Parents must not be intimidated by such terminology. If they are to gain a thorough understanding of their child's situation, they must look at his or her difficulties from all angles and evaluate how they affect every aspect of life, not just in school, but in relationships with other children and with the family. Learning disabilities do not interfere with just reading, writing and math. They affect play activities, communication and tasks at home.

Parents must become knowledgeable about their child's specific problems so they can help him or her obtain all the services needed. They must learn how to organize their child's life so as to maximize his or her strengths and enable him or her to enjoy the greatest variety of successful experiences.

Learning disabilities can appear in any area of the learning process and can be manifested in different ways.

Input or Perception Disabilities

Information enters the brain through all five senses. In learning, the most important senses are seeing and hearing. *Input* does not refer to the physical recording of information by the eye or ear, but rather to how the brain processes what is seen or heard. This process of perceiving the world is called *perception*. A perception disability can be visual or auditory.

---

3. The information in this section has also been taken from *ADHD: Attention Deficit-Hyperactivity Disorder and Learning Disabilities* and has been reproduced with minor adaptations.

Visual Perception Disabilities (1)

A child might confuse visual input, reversing letters—like ꙅ for *e*—or have trouble distinguishing *d* and *b* or *p* and *q*. *Was* might be read as *saw* or *dog* as *god*. This confusion might show up in written work, copied designs or tasks in which the eyes have to guide the hands (visual-motor tasks). Children with visual-motor problems might have difficulty catching or kicking a ball, doing puzzles, hammering a nail, skipping rope, etc.

There are other types of visual perception disabilities. For example, some children might have difficulty orienting themselves in space or telling left from right. Others might have "figure-ground" difficulties, that is, they might have difficulty focusing on one specific thing rather than on the entire background. For example, when reading, they might skip words or lines. Judging distance is another visual perception task. Children might misjudge depth and bump into things or miss the top step of the stairs. They might seem careless, knocking over a glass because they misjudged the distance and their hand got there too soon.

Auditory Perception Disabilities (2)

Some children have difficulty distinguishing subtle differences in sounds. They might misunderstand what someone is saying to them, because they confuse words, like *blue* and *blow* or *ball* and *bell*, and thus respond incorrectly.

Some children have difficulty with auditory "figure-ground". For example, a boy might be watching television in a room where others are playing. His mother is in another room and says, "Come in and set the table". She might not be "heard" because her son could not separate her voice (the figure) from the other sounds (the background). It might seem that he never listens.

Some children cannot process sound input at a normal speed. They always seem to miss part of what people are saying to them. You must speak slower if you want them to understand or ask them to repeat what you have said.

Integration Disabilities

Once information is recorded, it must be placed in the correct order (sequencing), understood in the context in which it is used (abstraction), and integrated with the other information processed by the brain (organization). A child can have difficulty in one or more of these areas. Problems occur primarily with visual or auditory perception. Parents might be told that their child has an auditory sequencing disability but is good at visual sequencing.

Sequencing Disabilities

A child might read or hear a story and understand it. But in retelling it or writing it down, he or she may confuse the sequence of events, starting in the middle, then going to the beginning, before winding up at the end. The child might see 23 but write it as 32. Spelling errors are common—all the letters may be there, but in the wrong order. Such children may be able to memorize a sequence, like the months of the year. But, if you ask what comes after September, they may not be able to find the place in the sequence, and will have to start with January and work their way down to September before they can answer. They may hit a baseball and run to third base, instead of first.

Abstraction Disabilities

Most people understand the meaning of words and phrases on the basis of how they are used. There is a difference in the meaning of *dog* in phrases like "look at the dog" and "you dog".

Some children have difficulty understanding these differences. They also have difficulty understanding jokes, puns and sayings, as they take words literally.

Organization Disabilities

Some children can process discrete pieces of information, but have trouble integrating the pieces into a whole picture. They may be able to answer the questions at the end of the chapter, but be unable to explain what the chapter was about. They may do well on multiple-choice questions (where they simply have to recognize items of information), but poorly on essay-type exams. These children may have difficulty organizing themselves. Their rooms may be a mess; their notebooks, crammed with papers in the wrong place. Their whole lives may be disorganized.

Memory Disabilities

Once information is recorded and integrated, it must be stored for later retrieval. In general, there are two types of memory: short-term and long-term. Short-term memory refers to information you remember while you are paying attention to it; for example, you might remember a telephone number the operator has just given you, but forget it if someone talks to you before you dial it. Long-term memory refers to information that you have stored after it has been repeated and that you can retrieve by thinking about it. A child's short-term memory disability may affect visual input but not auditory, or vice versa.

A child with a memory disability may go over a spelling list and have it down pat (while he or she is concentrating on it), yet forget it by the next morning. The teacher might explain a math concept in school and the child understands it (while attending to it), yet comes home that night and forgets how to do the problem. In contrast, he or she might remember in great detail something the family did two or three years ago. There is no problem with long-term memory. However, the child may need to go over something ten or more times to remember it, whereas normally it should take three to five times.

Output Disabilities

Information is communicated through words (oral language) or through muscle activities such as writing, drawing or gesturing (motor skills). A child can have one or both of these output disabilities.

Oral Language Disabilities

We use two types of oral language: spontaneous (when we initiate a conversation) and demand (when someone asks us a question). With spontaneous language, we organize our thoughts and find the words we want before we speak. With demand language, we must do all of this as we speak.

A child may have a demand language disability. What is confusing is that when the child speaks (spontaneous language), he or she sounds normal. Yet, when asked a question (demand language), "Where's your sister?", "What did you do today?", the child will respond with "Huh?" or "What?" or ask you to repeat the question. If the child replies, he or she may ramble or have trouble finding the right words.

Motor Disabilities

A child may have difficulty using his or her large muscles (gross motor disability) or small muscles (fine motor disability). A child with gross motor problems may be clumsy, stumble, or have trouble walking, running, climbing or riding a bike.

A child with a fine motor disability may have difficulty coordinating a group of small muscles, such as those in his or her dominant hand when writing. Such children will have slow, poor handwriting. They may hold their pen or pencil awkwardly and their hands will tire from the effort. They say their hand doesn't work as fast as their head and feels like a mitt. They may also have difficulty dressing, buttoning, tying or zipping.

Summary

It's crucial for parents to discover the areas in which their child has learning disabilities and to understand the extent to which these problems interfere with schoolwork, sports, and relationships with friends and family members. It's equally important for parents to recognize their child's skills and abilities, so they can learn how to help their son or daughter compensate for weaknesses by building on strengths.

Famous People with Learning Disabilities

Henry Adams, historian; Hans Christian Andersen, author; Harry Anderson, actor; John James Audubon, American naturalist and painter; Ann Bancroft, first woman to reach the North Pole by dog sled; Janette Bertrand, Quebec TV personality; Neils Bohr, physicist, theory of the structure of the atom; Cher, singer and actress; Winston Churchill, British prime minister; Harvey Cushing, brain surgeon; Tom Cruise, actor; Charles Darwin, English naturalist; Leonardo da Vinci, artist and architect; Frank Dunkle, director of U.S. Fish & Wildlife Service; Thomas Edison, inventor; Paul Ehrlich, bacteriologist; Albert Einstein, scientist; Dwight Eisenhower, U.S. president; Whoopi Goldberg, actress; William James, psychologist; Bruce Jenner, Olympic champion; John F. Kennedy, U.S. president;

Robert Kennedy, U.S. senator; Greg Louganis, Olympic champion; Abbott Lawrence Lowell, president of Harvard University; Amy Lowell, poet, sister of Lawrence Lowell; George S. Patton IV, U.S. army general; Auguste Rodin, sculptor; Nelson Rockefeller, governor, U.S. vice president; Richard Strauss, composer; Robert Rauschenberg, painter; Eero Saarinen, architect; Woodrow Wilson, U.S. president; Henry Winkler, actor.

Remember

- Learning disabilities are persistent and permanent. Through early detection and appropriate intervention, children will develop ways to compensate for their difficulties.
- An estimated 10 to 15 percent of the population has learning disabilities.
- People with learning disabilities have an average or above-average IQ.
- Parents are not the cause of their child's learning problems.

CHAPTER 2

SPECIFIC LEARNING DISABILITIES [4]

▼

The most common learning disabilities include dyslexia, auditory processing deficit, language disorders and attention deficit disorders.

Dyslexia

Dyslexia [5] is usually defined as a learning disability characterized by lasting problems with written language, including reading as well as writing and spelling, in children and adults who:

- have been raised in a normal emotional, social and cultural environment
- have received adequate instruction

---

4. The information in this chapter is based, in part, on publications by various organizations: an article by Brigitte Stanké on dyslexia as characterized by a lack of phonological awareness in children and adults, published by LDAQ; material by APEDA France (an association of parents of children with oral and written language disorders); and a working document on attention deficit hyperactivity disorder (ADHD) and the use of central nervous system stimulants, by the Quebec Department of Education.

5. *Dyslexia-dysgraphia* is also used to refer to both areas of skill difficulty — reading and writing.

- have a normal IQ, but whose written language skills are clearly inferior to their skills in other areas
- do not have a sensory impairment (visual, auditory)
- do not have major psychological problems.

This definition, however, is not particularly satisfactory: it mentions only the most general symptoms of the dyslexic-dysgraphic condition and fails to mention the causes. It suggests that if people's written language problems cannot be explained by social or economic difficulties, inadequate education, low intelligence, poor hearing or eyesight, or psychological or emotional problems, then they must be dyslexic.

There are two other definitions of dyslexia which are commonly used: the first, like the one above, is exclusionary and the second, which is more current, is inclusionary.

Exclusionary Definition

In 1968, the World Federation of Neurology defined *dyslexia* as a disorder that is manifested by difficulty in learning to read despite conventional instruction, adequate intelligence and socio-cultural opportunity, and that is dependent upon fundamental cognitive disabilities which are frequently of constitutional origin.

The proponents of this definition generally consider a lag of 12 to 18 months behind the educational standard to be significant for children under 9.

The general criticism of this definition is that it provides causes that exclude dyslexia. Moreover, the measurement used by its proponents suggests that parents have to wait until their child starts school and experiences significant reading difficulties before the problem can be diagnosed.

Inclusionary Definition

Exclusionary definitions being considered unsatisfactory, researchers have developed inclusionary definitions that underscore factors observed in reading disorders. Their studies have identified the strengths and weaknesses of children with a reading handicap. According to the research committee of the Orton Dyslexia Society, *dyslexia* can be defined as a specific language-based disorder of constitutional origin which is characterized by decoding difficulties resulting from a **phonological processing deficit**. Such decoding difficulties often exceed what is usually expected given the child's age and other cognitive academic abilities, and are not the result of generalized developmental delay or sensory impairment.

This definition suggests that dyslexia is manifested in variable difficulties with different forms of language, which generally include reading, writing and spelling, and that it is a much broader problem than a reading-related disorder. It clarifies that dyslexia is a language development disability which is due to a PHONOLOGICAL PROCESSING DEFICIT.

Manifestations

The most frequent anomalies resulting from dyslexia (reading disability) are manifested in decoding problems, comprehension difficulties, or both.

The most common decoding problems are:
- auditory or phonetic confusion (spagetti/spadetti)
- reversals (pacific/sapific)
- omissions (gasoline/gasline)
- additions (odor/order)
- substitutions (dress/drest)
- slow, hesitant, choppy, syllable by syllable reading

- difficulty dividing words into syllables
- lack of awareness of punctuation.

Individuals with dyslexia may grasp only part of the meaning of what they read or none at all. They do not like reading and often avoid subjects or activities that require reading. Most people with dyslexia have both decoding and comprehension disabilities.

The most frequent anomalies resulting from dysgraphia (writing disability) are manifested in:

- spelling mistakes and writing difficulties similar to those found in dyslexia
- other writing-specific problems (encoding, i.e. putting sound and symbol together)
- word transcription errors (getting lost when copying words from a book to paper)
- dropping of syllables (receive/reve)
- arbitrary or no word divisions (didn't believe me/didnt-pleveme)
- omissions (night/nite)
- grammatical errors
- slow, hesitant, poor writing.

Causes

Neuroscience, specifically neuropsychology, has provided the most valuable insight into the mechanisms of human language which are located at a "superior" level of general brain functioning. These mechanisms are highly complex and involve numerous brain functions. Dyslexia and dysgraphia are due to the poor functioning of the fundamental mechanisms responsible for written language, and specifically for:

- reading and comprehension

- concentration, memory, concepts of space and time, logic, sequencing, abstraction, etc.

Severe cases of dyslexia-dysgraphia are generally manifested as soon as the child starts school, whereas more mild cases can go unnoticed for a long time and not become obvious until later on.

Written language disorders are internationally recognized and classified by the World Health Organization (WHO). It is estimated that written language disabilities, including mild ones, affect between eight and ten percent of children in regular education programs and three to four times as many boys as girls. This frequency has remained stable over time, according to the data available, and applies to all populations.

Detection and Diagnosis

It is essential that detection take place as early as possible, preferably as soon as the child starts school. This way, the signs of difficulties that may arise when the child begins to learn written language skills can be identified. The child should be monitored closely throughout primary school to ensure that he or she does not suffer constant failure.

Detection should not be the responsibility of the school alone. The parents, family, family doctor and teacher must all collaborate in this fundamental task.

Dyslexia is one of the main causes of failure in school, and later in work and in relationships. In many cases, the attitudes and approaches taken by the family, school and work environment are inappropriate. A downward spiral begins: the child comes to dislike writing and develops an aversion for subjects that require reading. He or she maintains poor language skills, works slowly, becomes fatigued, and has difficulty writing down his or her thoughts and understanding what others are saying. It is therefore crucial that dyslexia be diagnosed early, the disorder be properly understood, and the child be given the appropriate tools to lighten the load and help him or her learn to live with the learning disability.

The diagnosis must be made by a specialist, as the nature, severity and context of the problems vary widely. Once the diagnosis has been made, a series of examinations will be conducted by different professionals. The number and type of examinations will depend on the complexity and severity of the problems.

Special Education

Dyslexic students must receive personalized special education —and speech therapy, if necessary—based on their strengths, weaknesses, interests and style of learning. Phonological assistance can be provided as early as kindergarten.[6] Special education assistance usually begins when the child starts first grade, to help the child learn written language basics. The special education program must be intensive and long enough to enable the student to develop skills and abilities.

Prognosis

How written language disabilities will evolve depends on many factors, which vary with the child and

- the type of dyslexia-dysgraphia
- the extent of the problem (severe problems are obviously more resistant to remediation)
- how early the problems are detected

---

6. *Phonology* refers to the treatment of sounds according to their function in language.

- the existence, regularity and intensity of special education, which may be needed for a number of years
- support given to encourage motivation, remedy past failures, rehabilitate written language skills, and modify behaviour at school, which is very often perceived as a place of punishment
- the attentiveness and cooperation of family members, the school and special educators.

With the proper treatment, environment and support, problems of dyslexia and dysgraphia will be alleviated, and can almost disappear if they are mild enough. In severe cases, written language skills will always remain weak, but written language performance will be considerably improved, thereby opening the door to valuable information and educational opportunities.

Auditory Processing Deficit

Children with an auditory processing problem can hear speech normally, but have difficulty processing sound—i.e. perceiving spoken language, interpreting it and retaining it.[7] They have problems with auditory memory and auditory attention. They need extra time to process auditory information before answering a question. They have trouble interpreting oral messages, understanding what has been said, and remembering directions.

Manifestations

There are a number of signs that can indicate an auditory processing disability. The child

---

7. See "Input or Perception Disabilities" in Chapter 1 for more detailed information.

- acts as if he or she has peripheral hearing loss, although hearing tests normal
- has difficulty understanding rapid speech
- needs a great deal of organization and structure in class
- has difficulty following complex instructions
- often asks people to repeat what they have said
- has a hard time learning to read and write
- often refuses to participate in class discussions or answers inappropriately
- is sulky or gloomy
- has little aptitude for music and singing
- has difficulty hearing and understanding in noisy surroundings.

Intervention

A number of general guidelines have been developed to improve communication in class with students who have an auditory processing disability.

Carefully Choose Where the Child Should Sit

All possible options should be reviewed when deciding where the child should sit in class. It is advisable to consider such factors as the acoustics of the classroom given the level of ambient noise and reverberation, the layout of the classroom, and the teacher's style of communication. Students with an auditory processing problem generally learn better in an enclosed classroom than in an open-plan environment.

In some cases, the audiology evaluation reveals a difference between the student's two ears in terms of central auditory capacity. Choosing a place in the classroom that will encourage use of the student's better ear is recommended. The audiologist can provide parents with information on the sound-filtering devices available.

Catch the Child's Attention

The teacher should always catch the student's attention before giving instructions in class. Calling the student by name or touching him or her gently will help the student focus on the matter at hand.

Check Comprehension

It is wise to ask the student questions on the topic of discussion to ensure that he or she is following and understanding.

Paraphrase and Repeat

Children with auditory perception disabilities should be encouraged to tell the teacher when they do not understand what is being explained. The teacher should not hesitate to rephrase a sentence: it may contain sounds or groups of sounds the child has difficulty differentiating or words he or she is unfamiliar with. Some students may also be suffering from language development delays. In either case, repetition is helpful.

Use Short, Simple Instructions

If instructions are overly long and complex, students with auditory memory problems will be completely lost.

Help the Child Prepare in Advance

Children who read in advance on a given topic will be more familiar with the new vocabulary and ideas covered in class and better able to participate in class discussions. Advance preparation is very important and can be supervised by the parents.

Prepare a Vocabulary List

Before the teacher introduces new ideas, he or she should write the new words that will be used on the board and start a discussion about them.

Establish Visual Reference Points

Visual references enable students to draw on their strengths and make the auditory-visual associations they often need to learn new ideas and words.

Provide the Student with Personalized Support

Students with auditory perception disabilities require individual attention. They must, insofar as possible, be given personalized support to help them bridge their language and comprehension gaps.

Set up Quiet Study Areas

It is important to create study areas that are free of visual and auditory distraction. This helps alleviate figure-ground discrimination problems.

Help All Parties Get Involved

The teacher should advise the other staff members and the parents about the subject of the vocabulary that will be covered in class so that their advance preparation complements class work.

Write Instructions on the Board

Students with auditory perception problems may have difficulty following oral instructions. Teachers can help by writing instructions on the board, so they can transcribe them in their notebooks. Teachers can also ask specific students to make sure the learning-disabled student has correctly understood what must be done that day.

Encourage Language Exercises

Expressive language exercises such as reading, conversation and role-playing should be encouraged. Reading is extremely important because it enables the student to fill in information he or she has had difficulty remembering because of a perception disability. Parents can provide invaluable support by signing their child up at a public library and pursuing expressive language activities at home.

Manage Energy

Students with perception disabilities tire more easily. They cannot always follow classroom activities on a continuous basis. Teachers should therefore alternate periods of intensive work with periods of relaxation, during which the student can move around the classroom.

Keep Parents Informed

Teachers must keep parents up to date on the situation at all times so they understand their child's successes and difficulties and the need for individual tutoring at home.

Evaluate Progress

It is important to evaluate the child's progress on a regular basis and not simply assume that the program is working. It is much wiser to make changes along the way than to wait until the child suffers yet another failure before taking action.

Language Disorders

Some problems encountered in school are due to early language development difficulties. Some children have difficulty developing and using language as a means of communication at a young age.[8] These children grapple with comprehension and expression problems and have trouble learning to read and write. While these problems are persistent, they are manifested in different ways as the child grows up.

The majority of reading-related disabilities are due to a language problem: 80 percent of children with learning disabilities experience problems as a result of delayed oral language development. These children may have receptive and expressive language problems and most of them have phonological processing problems.

Difference between Language Delay and Language Disorder

A "language delay" is a lag in comparison with the normal language development curve for reception or expression or both, and is related to the child's particular situation, e.g. social deprivation, multilingualism, low IQ, hearing impairment, repeated ear infections, etc.

A "language disorder" is reflected in a departure from the normal language development curve and is characterized by atypical development. Language acquisition is unusual and cannot be compared with normal development. Language disorders do not have an apparent cause, cannot be explained by a low IQ, hearing impairment or emotional problems, and are permanent. If the disorder is mild, the problem will not

---

8. Language disorders are divided into three categories: form (speech sounds, grammar); content (meaning of words); and use (utilization of language to ask questions, seek answers, express thoughts in conversation, etc.).

necessarily be detected in the first years of the child's life and the signs may not become obvious until the child studies written language.

Manifestations

Language disorders are generally manifested in children with learning disabilities as:

- an inability to concentrate on an oral message or understand it, if it is given quickly
- difficulty expressing ideas orally that seem to have been understood
- difficulty speaking their mother tongue with adequate grammatical ease
- difficulty holding or following a conversation on an unfamiliar subject
- difficulty following the right order of events when telling a story
- difficulty following oral or written directions.

Dysphasia

Language disorders include a specific language deficiency known as *dysphasia*, which is always accompanied by learning disabilities. Dysphasia is a developmental language disorder. According to Dr. Isabelle Rapin, dysphasic syndromes are characterized by significantly delayed acquisition of language, despite

- normal hearing
- normal non-verbal intelligence
- the absence of severe brain damage
- a stimulating language environment.

Dysphasia can be summarized as follows:

- it is a type of learning disability that affects primarily language
- children with the problem have normal IQs
- dysphasia is a permanent disorder that has repercussions on the child's emotional, social, family and academic life; these repercussions are all the more serious since the problem is little known
- the extent of the problem is variable (mild, moderate, severe)
- the problem can be manifested in different ways as the child grows
- there are no medications or surgical procedures that can be used to treat dysphasia. The evaluation is performed by a multidisciplinary team (psychologist, speech therapist, audiologist and pediatric neurologist). The diagnosis must be made by a speech therapist since the problem is a language disorder.
- The only possible treatment is special education and assistance in developing visual means of compensation. Special education training is required in school; often the aid of a psychomotor expert, occupational therapist and psychologist is also required.

Cause of Dysphasia

Researchers agree that dysphasia is neurologically based. Some researchers believe that people suffering from dysphasia are "brain different". Other researchers maintain that dysphasia reflects a variety of dysfunctions in the brain pathways required for language comprehension, development and programming. The nature of these dysfunctions is unknown; the cause, in most cases, is a genetic problem or a lesion appearing in the developing brain (during pregnancy, anoxia during child-birth, and so on).

The problem exists at birth; it does not occur after birth as a result of emotional or other trauma. Standard neurological tests do not necessarily provide information on the condition. Long-term observation and the pooling of data by all those involved are, still today, the only real ways of determining the presence and impact of the disorder.

Oral language deficiency of a dysphasic nature affects written language, i.e. reading and writing, to varying degrees. When dysphasia is mild, it cannot be detected at a early age because the signs are too inconspicuous; they usually do not become apparent until the child begins school.

Children affected by mild or moderate dysphasia can function in a regular classroom, with speech therapy and special education support. Children with moderate to severe disabilities of this nature may be placed in special language classes.

Intervention

A number of approaches are used to promote communication with young children suffering from dysphasia. They include:

- getting the child's attention by calling his or her name or touching him or her gently
- choosing a topic that arouses the child's interest
- adapting your way of speaking to the child's level of language
- speaking slowly, using only a few words at a time, and articulating clearly
- not hesitating to repeat yourself several times
- using intonation, gestures and context
- encouraging the child to use only one language

- establishing a good relationship and having fun with the child, using all forms of communication (gestures, looks, etc.). Without communication, the child cannot learn.
- encouraging the child to develop compensation strategies, by building on the child's strengths
- using visual media to promote communication
- putting the child in daycare at an early age to encourage him or her to develop compensatory strategies.

Other approaches can be used to promote verbal comprehension in school, such as:

- ensuring the student thoroughly understands the vocabulary used in class (and giving the parents a vocabulary list)
- preparing definitions of or illustrations for unfamiliar words or specific expressions
- reinforcing verbal messages through visual means: signs, gestures, facial expressions, illustrations, written words, etc.
- using visual material to illustrate ideas, directions, procedures and activities, and thus emphasize the topic being discussed in class
- illustrating the class routine with pictograms
- making audio recordings of the teacher's presentations (to replace course notes)
- giving clear, concise and orderly explanations in class
- providing a course outline
- addressing the child directly by calling him or her by name, making eye contact or touching the child when explaining something or giving instructions to the group
- checking whether the student has understood by asking him or her to restate what has been said

- adapting what you say (content) and how you say it (form) to the student's level of comprehension
- associating verbal information with specific objects, actions and events to encourage greater comprehension; using concrete material and illustrating explanations with demonstrations
- avoiding excessive auditory, visual and verbal stimulation, e.g. continuous background noise
- planning a moment's silence in class after an activity requiring comprehension, or alternating activities requiring comprehension with others that do not
- speaking more slowly
- repeating or reformulating what you have said
- articulating clearly
- keeping sentences short
- reinforcing comprehension, by alluding to the child's experience, situations in his or her everyday life, personal objects or photos, then moving gradually away from them. Providing examples after presenting a new idea.

Attention Deficit Disorder and Attention Deficit Hyperactivity Disorder

Attention deficit disorder (ADD) and *attention deficit hyperactivity disorder* (ADHD) refer to a group of symptoms that include inattention, hyperactivity and impulsivity.

Children with ADD have trouble paying attention and concentrating. At school, when they try to sit still and listen, they become mentally fatigued and bored. At home, it seems as though they willfully refuse to listen to their parents. They have difficulty completing a task, unless it is of particular interest to them. Their minds are racing and wander easily; they are dreaming when they are supposed to be doing schoolwork or other activities such as putting away their toys. In general, these children are easily distracted and, because they are impulsive, they do things quickly, without thinking. They often give the impression that they are badly behaved and disorganized.

Children with ADHD are continually on the go, as if driven by a motor. They have difficulty sitting still; they are constantly moving around. They may be socially immature and moody. It is very difficult to satisfy them because they always seem to be looking for something. They are often thought to be inconsistent because they can do something one day and suddenly not be able to do it the next.

According to the *Diagnostic and Statistical Manual of Mental Disorders* published by the American Psychiatric Association (4th edition, 1994, Washington, DC), children with ADD or ADHD suffer from inattention or hyperactivity/impulsivity more persistently and more severely than other children at a similar level of development.

Psychologist Dr. Russell A. Barkley maintains that ADD and ADHD are due to a delay in the neurological development of the inhibition of responses to the different stimuli bombarding the child, which results in inefficiency in fundamental neuropsychological functions affecting self-control and future-oriented behaviour. This deficit is related to executory functions apparently based in the frontal regions of the brain. ADD and ADHD are therefore not due to the parents' personality or the child's character, maturity or willingness. These problems have a physical basis; while they cannot be cured, they can be controlled.

ADD and ADHD are the most frequently diagnosed problems in North American children: this is very controversial because there is no specific biological indicator to confirm diagnosis. Researchers have found that the condition tends to run in families, but have not yet isolated the gene responsible.

It is estimated that three to five percent of children suffer from ADD or ADHD. These disorders affect both boys and girls, and appear before the age of seven. Twenty-five percent of children with ADD or ADHD also have learning disabilities, causing a lag in oral language, reading, writing and arithmetic.

Diagnosis

A differential diagnosis is complex and requires a careful multidisciplinary evaluation. Each specialist uses the tools he or she deems appropriate. New tests are constantly being developed and existing tests improved. Tests, in the absence of standards, are used to observe the subject's behaviour, how he or she solves problems and the type of errors he or she makes, so that the child's deficits can be identified.

Intervention

The treatment for ADD and ADHD includes special education, behavioural training and medication.

Medication

Methylphenidate, marketed under the name "Ritalin", is the medication most often used to counteract the symptoms of ADD and ADHD. It is a central nervous system stimulant, which increases attention span and concentration and decreases impulsivity. The tendency to prescribe methylphenidate for ADD and ADHD is specific to North America. In other countries, it is prescribed in less than 0.5 percent of cases. When prescribing a medication, the doctor (pediatrician, neurologist, psychiatrist or general practitioner) generally takes into account the symptoms, behaviour, learning problems and confirmation of the ADD or ADHD diagnosis.

Some specialists, in particular in Belgium, approach the problem from a cognitive perspective, trying to describe the child's various deficits rather than labeling him or her ADD or ADHD. In future, this approach may allow for different means of treating children with ADD only and offer a viable alternative to medication.

Some experts believe that medication alone is sufficient to help these children, whereas others believe that a multimodal approach is essential to their development. Clinical experts as well as parents are therefore faced with a dilemma: deciding whether to use medication to reduce symptoms related to ADD or ADHD. This dilemma must be solved quickly: statistics indicate that the use of medication has been constantly on the rise since 1990. Close collaboration among the different specialists is therefore necessary to resolve the controversy surrounding the question of medication.

One thing is certain: positive changes are often seen in the behaviour and academic performance of children taking methylphenidate.

Multimodal Approach

The multimodal approach recommended by many specialists includes changes in the way the classroom is organized, meetings with the family to demystify the problem, cognitive and behavioral psychotherapy or psychodynamics, and training in social skills.

The ADD or ADHD diagnosis is complex because, as mentioned, there is no specific biological marker to confirm it. The condition can vary from mild to severe. Differentiating children suffering from this problem from those who do not can be very difficult.

Parents lack knowledge and all too often have to rely on the media for information on the problem. This can create confusion and erode confidence in the professionals working with their children. Parents should always feel free to ask questions and consult a number of professionals, if need be.

Remember

- Dyslexia is a reading-related learning disability that occurs despite normal intelligence. It is due to a specific language disorder, the cause of which is a phonological processing deficit.

- An auditory processing deficit cannot be detected until an evaluation has been conducted by speech therapists and audiologists specializing in such problems.

- Among children with learning disabilities, some 80 percent suffer from delayed oral language development. These children may have difficulties understanding language and expressing themselves. Most have phonological processing difficulties.

- The ADD or ADHD diagnosis cannot be made until a thorough evaluation is conducted by specialists. Treatment includes educational assistance, behavioural training, and medication, if necessary.

CHAPTER 3

EVALUATION OF LEARNING DISABILITIES

▼

Purpose of the Evaluation

Parents who believe their son or daughter has a learning disability should not hesitate to take him or her to the family doctor for a physical examination or to arrange a meeting with the teacher to discuss the difficulties the child is encountering. If an evaluation proves necessary, they can take part in it along with the required professionals. While they are waiting for the evaluation date, they should find out all they can about the process and what the anticipated outcome may mean.

The purpose of the evaluation is to discover whether the child has learning disabilities, identify the child's strengths and weaknesses, and establish the educational programs and services that will meet his or her needs.

Parents will experience a wide range of emotions when they embark on the process of having their child evaluated or tested to determine his or her academic and psychological profile. But the evaluation should give them answers that will help them understand the child's problems and see what can be done to improve the situation.

The evaluation process can be initiated by a parent or at the recommendation of the school. It is important to note that a evaluation cannot be undertaken without the parents' consent.

If an evaluation is suggested by the school — and carried out with the parents' consent — it is free of charge. However, parents do not have a say in the choice of evaluator when the school initiates the process. Moreover, the waiting list can be long. If, for one reason or another, parents are unable to obtain an evaluation through the school system, they can go to a hospital or, in Québec, to a local community services center. They must realize that the wait at these organizations can be long as well. Parents can also approach private-sector organizations, but must first consider the following questions:

- Does the professional being consulted have an adequate knowledge of learning disabilities?
- Will the school reimburse the cost of the evaluation?
- Will the school accept the results of the tests?
- Will their private health insurance cover all or a portion of the costs?

What the Evaluation Involves

The evaluation is generally performed by health and education professionals. It usually includes:

- an interview with the parents or family
- a complete case history, and information on the difficulties
- a medical examination
- psychological, speech and academic examinations
- an audiology examination.

Role of the Multidisciplinary Team

The **pediatrician** is a physician specializing in overall child development. He or she will begin by evaluating the child's health. If necessary, the pediatrician will refer the child for additional testing of eyesight, hearing, language skills, etc.

Other specialists, such as a neurologist and child psychologist, may also be involved in the evaluation, especially in cases where the child shows signs of ADD or ADHD.

The **psychologist** is the professional who evaluates the child's intelligence and learning styles. Intelligence tests are used to determine the child's overall ability to learn and will indicate how the child learns best, i.e. by reading, hearing information or handling objects. Achievement tests are used to discover what the child has learned so far in school subjects, such as reading, spelling, arithmetic, and to assess the child's general knowledge.

The **speech therapist** evaluates the child's oral communication skills, and formally determines the child's level of oral expression and comprehension in order to check the impact on the child's learning.

The **special education teacher** evaluates the nature of the learning disabilities in school in order to establish a special education plan to remediate or compensate for the difficulties.

The **audiologist** evaluates central and peripheral auditory problems and assesses how these problems affect learning.

The **teacher** plays an important role in the evaluation process, because he or she sees the child regularly in an environment where other children the same age are developing. Teachers can use classroom observations and academic records to informally assess children who they feel may have learning disabilities because of the discrepancies in academic performance or social difficulties.

Parents play a key role in the evaluation of their child because

- they know their child better than anyone else

- they are able to compile a great deal of information about their child
- professionals may come and go, but parents are always there.

The parents should start a personal file with as much information about their child as possible. The file should include:

- report cards
- the pediatrician and family doctor's report
- specialists' reports
- personal observations.

Presentation of Results

When parents receive the results of their child's evaluation, they should note any technical terms they do not understand and ask for a clear explanation of the disability their child is experiencing. They should feel free to ask for further information on their role in helping their child. A parent should preferably be accompanied by his or her spouse or a friend when the results are presented.

It is not easy to diagnose a learning disability or prescribe the right treatment, because there is never a single well-defined cause. It is unlikely that two children with learning disabilities will display exactly the same symptoms. Every child is strong in some areas and weak in others. For example, a nine-year-old with learning disabilities may have a very high IQ, but be lagging behind his or her group by two to three years.

The evaluation may not address all the questions and concerns of parents about their child's learning disability. Parents are often disappointed that the evaluation does not offer a clear-cut solution to their child's problems. It is important to consider the evaluation results and recommendations as a starting point for assistance. Parents must be receptive to the suggestions made, because the evaluation is the first step in a long process aimed at helping their child develop his or her strengths. And they will need help along the way. Even if the parents do not completely agree with the evaluation results, they should take the results into account because they provide information from a reliable source.

All children with a learning disability need special educational assistance. The basic principle is to build on the child's strengths, while reinforcing means of improving, getting around or compensating for the child's weaknesses. Newly developed special education techniques often prove very beneficial for the child.

Word of Warning about Intervention

What decision should parents make about the various treatments recommended? When a treatment is recommended for a child, the parents obviously feel very vulnerable because they want the best for their son or daughter. In this decision, as in many others, the rule of thumb is to use common sense and to think twice before starting something new. Treatments that are not recommended by the physician or specialist— or that they are unfamiliar with—may seem promising, but often have not been researched and studied in-depth. Moreover, some of these treatments can be very costly. In any case, parents should discuss the different therapies as well as their risks and benefits with their doctor. The local chapters of learning disabilities associations are often good sources of information in this regard for parents and their doctors.

Medication is sometimes prescribed for children with a behaviour problem or an attention deficit. Some medications, such as psychostimulants (like Ritalin), should be considered only in very specific cases and solely on a doctor's recommendation.

After parents become familiar with the different types of learning disabilities and the terms used to describe them, they need to gather information on their child's specific handicaps and learn how to recognize his or her strengths and skills in order to emphasize them. The parents will work in close collaboration with the school in deciding on the necessary measures. But they must come to an agreement with the specialists on three points: the nature of the problem or the diagnosis, the level of assistance required, and where help can be obtained.

Some children can benefit from a special education program tailored to their needs, while continuing to attend regular classes. Others do better receiving special classes at school for part of the day, then joining their regular class for the rest. Still other children must attend classes at a special school. Regardless of the special education, the objective of any program is to provide the child with education adapted to his or her abilities, and to help the child overcome or compensate for weaknesses.

Most children with learning disabilities continue to experience these problems through adolescence. It is therefore important for parents to work on a continuing basis with the school to set up special education programs for the future.

Remember

- The evaluation is the first step in obtaining the assistance the child needs.

- If parents do not understand the technical terms used by the specialists or professionals conducting the evaluation, they should ask questions and take notes.

- It is important to emphasize the child's strengths and not just dwell on his or her weaknesses.

- Collaboration of the parents, health professionals and school is crucial.

- There is no miracle cure for learning disabilities.

CHAPTER 4

THE LOSS OF A DREAM

▼

You're going to have a child. You start making plans for the future. But, after your child is born and develops normally for a while, he or she starts showing signs of problems. Parents, thinking that their dream had come true, find this very hard to accept. They have to face not only their own preconceptions, but also those of society. In some cases, the professionals offering parents support have difficulty doing so because they have preconceptions of their own.

Parents are generally the first to notice that there is something different about their child's behaviour or the way he or she learns. The signs can be subtle and sometimes the learning disability does not become obvious until the child is exposed to complex tasks at school.

In accepting the fact that "something is wrong with the child", families undergo a difficult process of developing strategies to adapt to the situation — a process that can take weeks or months. For some families, the stress is more than they can bear. The news about their child can have a significant impact on each parent, the relationship between them, and their relationship with their child, friends, family and society in general.

Parents usually try to cushion themselves from the reality of this situation which upsets their plans for the future. Some hope for a miracle cure. But, in time, parents generally come to adopt a more positive, balanced outlook.

Stages Parents Go Through after the Diagnosis

Initially, the discrepancy between dream and reality is a shock. Parents experience the loss of a "normal" child. They are plagued by questions without answers, and feel upset, lost and confused. They deny the fact; they wish the situation were different and their worries would disappear. This stage is necessary, because it acts as a buffer or defence mechanism against a harsh reality.

Then comes despair mixed with anger, anxiety and sadness. They perceive the situation as unfair. "Why us?" They feel guilty, look for the cause, someone to blame, and feel like bad parents. They feel incapable of finding a solution and vent their anger and frustration on their professionals, family and friends. This is their way of defusing the aggressiveness they feel toward their child.

This is followed by a period of detachment or adaptation. Parents start to accept the situation and organize themselves accordingly. Their negative feelings are not completely in check, but this step leads little by little to acceptance and reorganization. The child will finally be recognized for who he or she is, with all his or her limitations and potential. The child takes his or her rightful place and is treated according to his or her needs like the other members of the family. At the same time, the parents become aware of their feelings toward their child. At that point, they become very determined to give their child every opportunity to blossom. Once parents have come to terms with the situation, they can draw lessons from the child's presence and condition. They often find a message in the situation that enables them to grow personally in terms of their values and priorities.

It's essential to bear in mind that the child is also sad about the situation and must mourn the fact that the evaluation process and educational assistance cannot provide a magic cure. Parents have the double challenge of dealing with their own emotions and those of their child.

Some Parents Ask for Help

Some parents say they need psychological support, especially when they're feeling angry and unsure. This assistance helps them, the child, and the brothers and sisters who are also going through emotional turmoil about the diagnosis.

Seeing Things from Another Perspective or "Welcome to Holland"

"I am often asked to describe the experience of raising a child with a disability to try to help people who have not shared that unique experience to understand it, to imagine how it would feel. It's like this:

"When you're going to have a baby, it's like planning a fabulous vacation trip to Italy. You buy a bunch of guidebooks and make your wonderful plans... the Coliseum, Michaelangelo's David, the gondolas of Venice. You may learn some handy phrases in Italian. It's all very exciting.

"After months of eager anticipation, the day finally arrives. You pack your bags and off you go. Several hours later, the plane lands. The stewardess comes in and says, 'Welcome to Holland.'

"`Holland?!´, you say, `what do you mean Holland? I signed up for Italy! I'm supposed to be in Italy. All my life, I've dreamed of going to Italy!´

"The stewardess replies, `There's been a change in the flight plan. We've landed in Holland and it is here you must stay.´

"The important thing is that they haven't taken you to a horrible disgusting, filthy place full of pestilence, famine and disease. It is just a different place. So, you must go and buy new guidebooks. You must learn a whole new language. You will meet a whole new group of people you would never have met. It is just a different place. It is slower-paced than Italy, less flashy than Italy, but after you have been there a while and you catch your breath, you look around and you begin to notice that Holland has windmills, Holland has tulips, Holland even has Rembrandts. But everyone you know is busy coming and going from Italy and they're all bragging about what a wonderful time they had there. And for the rest of your life you will say, `Yes, that's where I was supposed to go. That is what I had planned.´

"The pain of that will never, ever, ever go away because the loss of that dream is a very significant loss. But if you spend your life mourning the fact that you didn't go to Italy, you may never be free to enjoy the very special, the very lovely things about Holland."[9]

---

9. This text was written by Emily Pearly Kingsley and appeared in the *Voice Ottawa Newsletter*, 1994.

Remember

- There are many stages families go through after the diagnosis of a learning disability: shock, denial, despair, anger, sadness and finally acceptance and reorganization.

- Both parents and the child go through a period of sadness and frustration before accepting the situation.

- Accepting the loss of a dream often means opening the door to new discoveries.

CHAPTER 5

LIVING WITH LEARNING DISABILITIES[10]

▼

Children with learning disabilities live with chronic stress. How could it be otherwise when they have problems accomplishing tasks as ordinary as reading and writing and when they have to expend enormous amounts of energy just getting organized while those around them manage to do so effortlessly?

Parents of a child with learning disabilities have to understand the stress their child is living with. Their role is to help lighten their child's load; one way of doing so is to create opportunities for the child to talk about his or her difficulties, frustrations and fears. Children who have this outlet are less inclined to lash out at their siblings or classmates.

Paradoxically, children who feel that their parents avoid talking about the learning disability in their presence may be overly fearful. It is up to parents to let their child know that a learning disability is nothing to be ashamed of or kept secret. Children with learning disabilities must feel they can talk frankly about their problems with their family and friends.

---

10. The information in this chapter and the next is taken, in part, from two publications by the Learning Disabilities Association of Canada: *A Guide to Understanding Learning and Behaviour Problems in Children* and *Advocating for Your Child with Learning Disabilities*.

Loss of Self-Esteem

Teasing children in public about their disability can damage their self-esteem. But gentle teasing by a family member ordinarily has the opposite effect: it makes them feel more secure and at ease with others. It is also a perfect chance for a child to acquire a sense of humour, which in turn can reduce the stress of daily life.

Parents must be aware of the fragility of their child's self-esteem, and make sure that they do something enjoyable with the child every day. This can be as simple as reading the comics together or recounting a personal anecdote. Children love to hear their parents tell stories about being clumsy themselves or forgetting to do something at work. Seeing that mistakes can be made even by the adults whom they love and who are successful in life makes children feel "normal", and this gives them a real sense of well-being.

Children who are rejected by their peers, have problems in school, are constantly scolded for being late or called lazy or clumsy will not have a good opinion of themselves and may tend to be depressed. Loss of self-esteem can be very hard for a child with a learning disability to deal with. One remedy is for parents to encourage their children to take part in activities that interest them. If the parents can afford it, they might give their children a membership at a gym or sports center or provide them with classes or lessons that allow them a chance to express themselves artistically. Remember, children with learning disabilities are often very creative.

Other ways of building a child's self-esteem are
- creating opportunities for the child to participate in a group with other children, to share and even to teach other children what he or she is learning

- sharing some private time with the child every day
- letting the child tell you about his or her day so you can help find solutions to any problems that arise
- encouraging the child to express his or her feelings so you can find out what he or she is thinking.

School looms very large in children's lives and the lives of their families. If a child with a learning disability gets lower than average grades, the parents take it as a personal failure, which erodes their own self-esteem. It is important for parents to react to the stress this causes by expressing their own feelings, confiding in friends, and taking part in activities they enjoy. Some parents find that physical activity is beneficial.

The Child's Fears

The family has changed considerably in recent years. Today, children live in families of all sizes and shapes (traditional, single-parent, blended, adoptive). Moreover, family problems are more frequent, and it is easy for children with a disability to feel responsible for situations as diverse as a parent's absence or illness, divorce or separation, or lack of financial resources. It is vital to be alert to children's fears ("Where's Daddy?", "Is Daddy coming home?", "Is Mommy going to die?") which they may be hiding or simply can't express directly because they are too young. Anxiety in children may be manifested as sleep disturbances or immature behaviour such as baby-talk, bed-wetting or soiling of underwear.

Parents must be sensitive to the fears, fantasies and misconceptions that are common among young children, particularly children with learning disabilities. Such children need to be reassured, to be told that their behaviour, worries and difficulties are not the cause of the family's problems. Of course family relations are put to the test when a child has a learning disability, but there is no reason for the family to be destabilized or torn apart by the situation.

Family Disagreements and Breakdown

Children need to know that people can be angry with one another and still go on loving one another, and that parents can have arguments without getting divorced. The main thing to keep in mind is that children must be told what the disagreement is about and what effects it may have on future events. When parents separate or divorce, children have to be allowed and encouraged to go on loving the absent parent. Children don't stop loving one of their parents just because the parents no longer love one another. And children need to know that they are going to continue being loved and cared for, no matter what the change in parental situation, income, living arrangements or job.

Divorce, separation, or parental abandonment are particularly difficult for children under eight because they are too young to understand the difference between permanent relationships and relationships that can be terminated. They don't yet realize that love between adults is much more fragile than the bond between parent and child. It is hard for them to understand that a separation may have positive aspects for the adults in question although it has none for them. For example, it is not easy for children who are hyperactive and disorganized to have to live by a different set of rules in each household, keep track of their possessions in two separate houses and make friends in two different neighbourhoods.

Moving into an adoptive or foster home or living through their parents' separation or divorce increases children's fears. Children with learning disabilities have trouble imagining the consequences of such a situation realistically, and this makes them feel even more vulnerable. When they realize they've lost contact with someone important to them, they can easily imagine that something terrible could happen to them at any moment. And they feel they have very little control over their lives.

Parents can use dolls or photograph albums to teach their children about human relationships and the difference between biological relationships, which are permanent, and acquired relationships, which can be broken off. Children can make their own photo albums, or make up and illustrate their own stories. They can be encouraged to talk about events they can foresee, such as spending time with the absent parent at a specific time of year. The planned date of a visit to the child's absent mother or father can be marked on a calendar and the days until the visit can be crossed off as they go by. Children can make up and illustrate their own story about what life will be like with one parent or in a foster home. These methods can all be useful in helping children deal with the problem of a broken home.

All children have a greater need for organization and supervision at times when their lives are changing and disrupted; this is particularly true of a child with a learning disability. During such times, it is necessary to make sure that children continue having social contact with other children. Ways a parent can help include assisting children in inviting their friends to their house or, if they like the idea, enrolling them in a club or gym. It is advisable to warn teachers about changes occurring in a child's life so that they are not surprised if at times the child becomes aggressive, hyperactive or distracted, or behaves immaturely.

Divorce, separation, death, illness, adoption or placement in a foster home are particularly traumatizing for children who have already experienced significant disappointments in their lives, such as academic failure or social problems. Nevertheless, with an adult's help, a child can learn to distinguish between real and anticipated losses, and to realize that love, affection and enjoyment are still possible even if the context has changed.

Making Friends

Having friends means learning to trust and to be trustworthy. Friendship also means testing others and trying to find the level of aggressiveness and impulsiveness they can tolerate. Friendship teaches us an enormous amount: that friends have to wait their turn, agree about what they think is acceptable, and be sensitive to the ideas and feelings of others. It also teaches us that everyone is unique; that there are some things a person is willing to give up and other things the person is not; that sometimes other people need our support and sometimes we need theirs. And when we disagree with our friends, we learn how to reconcile with them through negotiation and compromise.

Children with learning disabilities often have trouble forming friendships with other children their own age. In general, young children can't be expected to be very sensitive to what other people want or feel, but children with a learning disability or short attention span have a greater tendency to be insensitive to others. Placed in a new situation or group of children, they may become overexcited and anxious.

These children have a hard time imagining what will happen when they get together with their peers. They may be afraid the situation will be as disastrous as similar situations in the past. Their level of anxiety rises, bad behaviour ensues, and the worst-case scenario is repeated. Parents' role is to diminish the level of complexity and amount of stimulation involved in social situations, and to have realistic expectations for their children.

Relationships with other people are by far the most important aspect of our lives. For young children, the most important people are their parents, but friendships with peers and other adults are also essential, and their importance increases as a child gets older. Children need to feel accepted by others, to feel part of a group, to feel their actions, hopes and goals are accepted and approved of by the people around them. They have to feel that they can count on other people for help, and that their friends in turn will ask them for help when they need it. They need friends who can share in their activities, sympathize with their feelings and talk about events they've shared.

No one needs hundreds of friends, but we all benefit from having a few true friends who care about us and enjoy our company. Parents should take time to encourage their child to be aware of the wishes and feelings of others and to act accordingly. Parents who teach their children to be sensitive to others leave them an invaluable legacy.

Around the age of six or seven, children with learning disabilities are ready to join a club or other group and participate in a community activity, provided the adult in charge or leader can help them feel comfortable and can manage to downplay their differences when they are with other children. In practice, this means that a group leader should never ask a child with a learning disability to read aloud, or expect the child to perform tasks requiring a great deal of coordination (tying knots or building complicated models, for example). The leader should replace competitive activities by cooperative ones, help the child with difficult tasks, and be alert to the child's frustration or excitement, which may involve being gentle with a frustrated child or finding a quiet corner for an overexcited one.

Parents of children with learning disabilities quickly learn that they can't compensate for all their children's weaknesses and that the road to success is not a smooth one. They also come to realize that some things can be negotiated while others require saying no. Parents should never allow their children to do whatever they like out of fear of provoking a tantrum or reluctance to endure their nagging or rebelliousness.

Success Stories

"When I think back on my childhood, I realize that my mother, father and two sisters gave me three things. First, I could see in their eyes that they loved me. The love I saw strengthened my identity. The second concerns the fact of being different. In my family, the fact that a person consulted a psychologist or couldn't read or write properly didn't make us treat the person with any less respect. Finally, while my parents always concentrated on my good qualities and strengths, we still worked hard on improving my grades in school.

"These three things helped me stay in school, pursue a career and establish a firm foundation of self-confidence. My parents also set an example for me. Being different is a good thing because I looked at things differently from my friends. I didn't have the same style they did, I had a different perception of things. This was valuable for me; it allowed me to develop as a unique person.

"When my parents looked into my eyes, I could see they loved me. Around the age of 10, I got 40% on a test; not having a good grade made me very sad. I remember my mother telling me, `40% is better than zero; now we're going to see how we can improve that grade'. When I was about eight or nine years old, I was good at organizing parties; my parents began letting me organize parties at our house. When I was 10 or 11, I liked downhill skiing, but there were two problems: first, I lived in Montréal, and second, my parents worked on Saturday and Sunday. It didn't take us long to solve these problems. Every week, they'd give me a small sum of money. I'd take the bus to the subway, then the subway to the station, where I caught the bus for Saint-Sauveur. When I arrived, I'd take a taxi to the ski slopes and spend the whole day there. Then I'd go home. Having this independence helped me develop self-confidence.

"Even though I didn't get good grades in school, the confidence my family gave me was an essential factor that enabled me to conquer my problems and go from success to success. At times, I'm full of uncertainty, but I have enough self-confidence to be happy."

Testimonial of an adult with a learning disability

* * *

"My parents knew I was intelligent, but they never imagined I had learning disabilities. They thought I was just being lazy. My mother was generally understanding, but my father wasn't. He thought I lacked motivation and failed because I wasn't working hard enough.

"The goals they'd set for me weren't impossible for someone with my talents, but because I was hyperactive and dyslexic, I couldn't achieve them. My parents' attitude contributed to my lack of self-confidence. Having other people think you're lazy is very bad for your ego.

"People should set goals for themselves which are based on their own interests, strong points and abilities instead of what others expect of them. My community college studies are an example of a goal I set for myself and achieved. I knew it would be hard. Of course I was prepared to take more than the required three years, but I was determined to succeed. I loved my program and the whole experience. It took me six years to earn a specialized engineering diploma, and despite being frequently advised to give up or change programs, I stuck with it, and have the diploma and five years' experience in the field. I'm no longer in that field today; I'm doing a different kind of work that's better suited to my abilities.

"I've learned another important lesson: when you have learning disabilities, you have to accept the situation and so do your parents. I was nearly in my twenties when my parents finally stopped thinking of my problems at school or at home as a handicap and understood that I learned differently because of the way my brain worked.

"I have a different, unique way of doing things. It may take me longer than someone else to perform a task, but I've found my own way of reaching my goals, and I can succeed as well and perhaps as easily as other people. The end justifies the means.

"Teach your children to develop their own strategies by telling them there are many ways to get around an obstacle and reach their goals. A straight line is not always the shortest path. In my case, I always try to get around any obstacles. When a problem seems too big, I break it down into smaller pieces so it's easier for me to find a solution.

"Later, my parents taught me to concentrate on my strong points. As a child, I didn't want to be constantly reminded of the subjects I failed (mathematics); I wanted to be congratulated on my academic successes, in history, geography, etc."

Comments of an adult with a learning disability and dyscalculia

Remember

- Children with learning disabilities live with chronic stress.

- It is vital to be aware of children's hidden fears.

- Divorce, separation, death, illness, adoption or placement in a foster home are particularly traumatizing for children who have already experienced major disappointments such as academic failure or social problems.

- With their friends, children learn to be sensitive to the ideas and feelings of others.

CHAPTER 6

PARENTAL ATTITUDES

▼

Being a parent is sometimes frustrating and often difficult, but it is also very gratifying. This is even truer when the child has a learning disability.

It is important for parents to make a point of having as many satisfying moments and occasions with their children as possible. This can mean simply doing things together that both parent and child enjoy, without worrying about skill, failure, or time limits.

What you do can be as ordinary as holding or hugging your child while telling a bedtime story, or singing while ironing or making dinner. What children mainly remember, and what they hold most dear, is sharing the experience with their parents.

Parents are in the best position to provide their learning-disabled child with constant, active support. It is up to them to help their child be successful in activities outside school and have positive rather than negative experiences at home and with friends. To achieve this, parents must be fully aware of their children's strengths and weaknesses. By helping their children develop their abilities and compensate for their disabilities, parents contribute to their children's self-confidence and positive image. Here are some winning strategies for achieving this.

Maintaining Close Supervision

Supervision is particularly necessary in the case of children with learning disabilities. Because they may have memory, organization, coordination or behavioural problems, these children need their time to be organized, so they know exactly when and where their everyday activities take place (meals, bath, chores, etc.) and can find their personal possessions easily.

Parents must quickly find ways of determining what their child needs to be more effective at a particular task (getting dressed, for example). Sometimes a task has to be simplified or divided into steps. Sometimes the child must be given one instruction at a time. As the child's skill increases, parental supervision can be reduced.

This approach gradually enables children to do things they weren't able to do before. But for it to be successful, parents must pinpoint what isn't working. Children may not understand what they are being asked to do; they may forget instructions; they may be distracted by something in their surroundings, such as their toys; or they may simply not know where to begin. Parents have to know the nature of the problem before they can find a solution.

The primary goal of parental supervision is always to help children find a framework in which they can function, so that little by little they become independent and able to plan activities and evaluate their performance themselves.

Distinguishing between Punishment and Discipline

Punishment involves constraint. It also makes children feel that they're "bad" and that adults are stronger than they are. Discipline, however, provides a model and inculcates values that make children eager to regain adults' good opinion of them. Discipline teaches children self-control; punishment does not.

Discipline involves setting an example, teaching, and expressing love and admiration. No one is as important to children as their parents or their usual caregivers. Children who feel accepted and admired by their parents and those around them are inclined to undertake difficult tasks and demonstrate self-discipline. Such undertakings are particularly challenging for children who are impulsive or are convinced they never do anything right and feel incapable of pleasing their parents.

When parents lose patience, when they express anger or frustration—which happens more frequently with a child who has a learning disability—they are not setting an example of the kind of self-discipline their child expects of them. It is always good to remember that self-discipline is a lifelong process.

Making Change Easier

Children with learning disabilities are rarely comfortable with unexpected change. Even pleasant surprises can upset them. They function best when everything is in its place and everything happens when it is supposed to.

Pre-school children with learning disabilities are generally capable of cooperating with their parents in organizing their bedroom and deciding where to put their trucks, dolls and clothing. By allowing children to take part in decision-making, parents teach them how to get organized by themselves. Children are never too young to learn this, or to decide, for example, what they should do first when tidying their room. They can even make a list of things to do and check them off when they're done. This encourages children to put their things away in the proper place so they're easier to find.

Using a list doesn't eliminate the need for parental supervision, but it does remind children what they have to do, so that parents don't have to repeat the same instructions over and over.

Decision-Making

Children with learning disabilities do much better when both parents hold the same views about acceptable behaviour and decide in advance what the consequences of unacceptable behaviour should be. It is not uncommon for parents to have different opinions on these questions, but it is much better for them to discuss their differences in private and agree ahead of time on a united plan of action.

All children must learn to negotiate what they want, instead of trying to get their way through tantrums, stubbornness, or refusal to participate. In family life, some things are negotiable and others are not. Even young children can understand that matters of health and safety are not negotiable. But there are some decisions that they can help make, such as whether they take their bath before or after supper or whether they would prefer a family picnic to dinner at a restaurant.

Weekly family meetings are ideal for getting everyone to talk about the week's events, share feelings and concerns, and collaborate in finding solutions. In the case of children with learning disabilities, weekly meetings are essential: they provide a chance to discuss how to deal with specific situations, recall solutions that have worked well and discard others. All the members of the family can ask for the help they need, whether it involves tying their shoelaces, drying the dishes or keeping from getting angry. Together, the family can choose the person to provide the help, and decide how often help is to be given.

Children who negotiate for something they want have an easier time realizing the role they play in achieving a result. Parents, for their part, must deal with problems one at a time and establish an order of priority; this means seeing to it that problems of health, safety and interpersonal relations are dealt with first. When one problem is solved, the next one can be concentrated on. In this way, parents teach their children to set priorities and make decisions.

Knowing How to Learn from Mistakes

Everyone makes mistakes. Instead of being considered failures or catastrophes, mistakes can be looked on as unique chances to learn something. In the case of children with learning disabilities, it is essential for parents to maintain this attitude. Because these children already have low self-esteem, parents should never hesitate to give them repeated encouragement along with any criticism.

Rather than comparing their child with other children the same age, parents should evaluate the child's progress by comparing it with his or her earlier achievements. The goal is to get the child to advance one step at a time from his or her current state of development to a higher level.

Parents who recognize their own imperfections are more likely to accept their child's, and are less prone to blame themselves for their child's disabilities or weaknesses. They understand that other people too have an effect on their child, that a child is the product of many factors (environment, temperament, personality, abilities, etc.).

With all children, and particularly children with learning disabilities, it is a mistake to make success the prime concern. Instead, parents should help their children find ways of functioning more effectively.

Maintaining a Good Attitude

While it is normal for parents to be discouraged and express their frustration when they find out their child has a learning disability, they ultimately have to accept the situation and do something about the problem; they can't stop living their lives because of it. It is vital for them to continue caring for the other children in the family, seeing their friends, and keeping some time and energy for the things that interest them.

Parents also have to realize that children do not necessarily understand the significance of the various events that occur in daily life; they depend on their parents to interpret them. If parents stress problems, mistakes and failures, their children will do the same.

Being Supportive

Parents provide their children with true support when they deal with things that are beyond the children's ability. They fulfil their role of protector by encouraging their children rather than blaming them, and by being the ones their children can always count on. But parents must also be careful to avoid dealing with a child's difficulties in a way that smothers the child. Maintaining this fine balance is an art, particularly when the child has learning disabilities.

As they grow up, children have less and less need for parents' constant presence and comfort; they have learned that their parents are there to listen to them and not judge them.

Providing children with support means being able to empathize with them. For example, it means recognizing that a task which is ordinarily easy to perform can be very difficult for a child with a learning disability. Children who are raised in a supportive and reassuring environment learn to be self-confident.

Being supportive means being sensitive to children's needs —for approval, help, independence, privacy—and knowing how to meet them.

Taking Siblings into Account

Brothers and sisters of children with learning disabilities also need to feel loved. They may feel that their sibling with special needs can get away with misbehaving or doing poor work, while they can't. Some are ashamed of their learning-disabled brother or sister. Others imagine they are the cause of the problem, or are afraid their own children will have similar problems later. And some are simply disappointed that a brother or sister with a learning disability can't take part in some of the activities they themselves enjoy.

Parents must not expect brothers and sisters to feel responsible for the child with learning disabilities. For example, there is no reason that siblings always have to include the learning-disabled brother or sister in their group of friends. They have the right to behave like children, have their own social life, and express feelings of guilt, frustration, disappointment and anger at times, just as their parents do.

Helping Children with Homework

Children with learning disabilities often have to work very hard in school just to earn a passing grade. Should they be asked to do homework too? Only a discussion between the parents and the teacher can provide an answer to this question. If the answer is affirmative, if the child really does need to do homework in order to progress, it is advisable to deal with it by establishing a simple routine and firm guidelines, and to keep in constant touch with the teacher.

Initially, until a routine is established, children should feel that their parents are there at all times. Later, parents can figure out ways to develop the children's independence gradually, until they are capable of doing their own work in their own work space, whether at a desk in their room or in a special nook reserved for them. It is also important that parents not take it upon themselves to finish a child's homework. Their role consists in encouraging their children, helping them with specific questions, developing their ability to communicate directly with the teacher, and offering them informed advice.

Parent Support Groups

These days, parents all too often don't have enough time to devote to their children, so they must constantly set priorities. One of these priorities should be their own self-development, so they can avoid dependence on outside solutions and reclaim their rightful area of jurisdiction as parents.

Being a parent is a career in itself. It is never an easy job, and it is even harder when your child is different from other children. In addition to self-development, parents should never hesitate to join a support group. By sharing their fears and triumphs with other parents, they can gain a better understanding of their own situation and thus take more effective action.

Other Sources of Aid

In addition to their parents' support, children with learning disabilities can benefit from the help of people outside the nuclear family. Grandparents, aunts, uncles and family friends can certainly help a child feel loved and confident. In general, adults with learning disabilities who have had successful lives attach a great deal of importance to the support they received in childhood from adults who were not part of their immediate family.

Parents of a learning-disabled child also need support from outside the immediate family. They need friends who will listen to them and understand them. Such friends don't need to be experts in the field; they just need to be there and be willing to listen.

Remember

- Proper supervision enables children to learn to do things they were unable to do before.

- Discipline, unlike punishment, provides a positive model, teaches children self-control and inculcates values that make them eager to gain adults' approval.

- If parents stress problems, mistakes and failures, the children will acquire the same attitude.

- Brothers and sisters of a learning-disabled child also require attention and need to feel loved.

- Parents should never hesitate to ask for help and use all available resources.

Chapter 7

Obtaining Services from the School System

▼

The role of parents of children with learning disabilities has many facets. In addition to providing their children with constant support, parents act as advocates to defend their rights and interests at the school they attend and the school board to which the school belongs.

Learning about Your Child's Rights

Section 10 of the Quebec *Charter of Rights and Freedoms* stipulates:

"Every person has a right to full and equal recognition and exercise of his (her) human rights and freedoms, without distinction, exclusion or preference based on ... a handicap or the use of any means to palliate a handicap. Discrimination exists where such a distinction, exclusion or preference has the effect of nullifying or impairing such right."

In addition, the *Charter* recognizes the right to information and the right to non-disclosure of confidential information. In practical terms, that means that you can have access to your child's school records and that its content cannot be communicated to anyone else without your consent.

The Quebec *Education Act* currently in force specifies the legal obligations of schools and school boards with respect to special services, student evaluation, and establishment of an individual education plan designed to meet the student's needs. It grants every educational institution functions and powers with regard to educational services, other student services and management of human, physical and financial resources. Since these functions and powers are administered by a school council, parent representation on this council is very important. Here are some relevant extracts from the *Education Act*.

Student's Right to Instructional Services and Special Education:

"Every person is entitled to the preschool education services and elementary and secondary school instructional services provided for by this Act and by the basic school regulation made by the government... Every person is also entitled to other educational services, student services and special educational services provided for by this Act... within the scope of the programs offered by the school board..." (Section 1)

"Every resident of Quebec is entitled to free educational services." (Section 3)

Student Evaluation:

"Every school board shall ... adapt the educational services provided to a handicapped student or a student with a social maladjustment or a learning disability according to the student's needs and in keeping with the student's abilities as evaluated by the school board according to the procedures prescribed..." (Section 234)

Individualized Education Plan:

"In the case of a handicapped student or a student with ... a learning disability, the principal, with the assistance of the student's parents, of the staff providing services to the student, and of the student himself, unless the student is unable to do so, shall establish an individualized education plan adapted to the needs of the student. The plan must be consistent with the board's policy concerning the organization of services for handicapped students and students with social maladjustments or learning disabilities and in keeping with the ability and needs of the student as evaluated by the school board before the student's placement and enrolment at the school." (Section 96.14)

Your Commitment as a Parent

Acting with Determination and Self-Assurance

As a parent, you are the permanent link between your child and the education system, and you know how much your child depends on what school provides. Sometimes teachers and other staff members leave to work elsewhere, or your child has to attend a different school. If you are informed that your child is having difficulties in school, if you notice this yourself, or if someone suggests that your child be placed in a special program, take time to think it over. It is important for you to understand the situation fully and take the most appropriate action.

Finding the Information

We advise you to start a personal file that contains as much information as possible about your child. The file should include report cards, which help in evaluating the progress your child is making in school; a report by the child's pediatrician or family doctor; and reports from other caregivers or special educators.

It is very important to include in this file your personal observations on your child's behaviour, strengths and weaknesses. These observations are particularly useful in preventing your child from being labelled lazy or irresponsible; such labelling can destroy a child's self-esteem.

It is essential that your child be directed toward a situation that will foster his or her fullest development and potential.

Taking Steps

The *Education Act* recognizes your right to be involved in your child's education plan. It is therefore advisable to establish a good relationship with the school staff members who will be providing your child with services; they are potentially your most valuable allies.

An interview with the teacher and the principal is always indicated. The meeting with the teacher will give you an opportunity to discuss your child's particular needs. Ask the teacher for specific information on the child's academic performance and behaviour. Work together to develop an appropriate system of communication and monitoring. If necessary, demand an evaluation by a special educator. Every school board is required to provide this service. Also, don't hesitate to ask for a meeting with the principal to decide on the direction your child's education should take.

When the learning disability has been identified, an individualized education plan must be established; the principal, staff and parents must work together to draw up the plan. As a parent, you are responsible for making sure the school principal sees to the implementation and periodic evaluation of your child's education plan.

The individualized education plan covers all the services the child will receive over a given period of time. It is a tool for planning and monitoring the educational measures that school and parents decide on together. It necessarily takes into account the child's evaluation and specific needs.

The purpose of the educational plan is to:

1. describe the child's level of performance when he or she starts receiving assistance
2. establish the objectives to be achieved
3. explain the measures to be provided to achieve these objectives
4. indicate how often meetings should be held to check on the child's progress and if necessary modify the measures being taken.

The last step is designed to ensure that the services your child is receiving are appropriate to his or her needs.

Establishing the education plan involves answering the following questions:

- What are the child's strengths and weaknesses?
- What are the educational goals to concentrate on during the year?
- What objectives should school staff pay particular attention to?
- What additional services does the student require to ensure his or her harmonious development?
- What human and physical resources are required to provide the child with help?
- To what degree can the child participate in school activities and regular class activities?
- Is the child capable of receiving the services he or she needs?
- What criteria will be used to evaluate the child's progress?

Implementing an individualized education plan requires a genuine commitment from everyone concerned. Parents' active participation is an essential component of its success.

It should be noted that in Quebec, the Department of Education grants additional credits to fund additional services (special education, speech therapy, etc.) for students with social maladjustments or learning disabilities.

Your child may also need tests and exams to be adapted. You can discuss the situation with the school principal. You should also be sure to get approval from your school board. You can obtain information from the regional office of the Department of Education responsible for adapted education.

When it comes to services that can be obtained in the school, you should be familiar with the Quebec Department of Education's interpretation of the definitions of a handicapped student or a student with a social maladjustment or learning disability (see Appendix 2, p. 111).

In every region, there are other resources beside those offered by the school; you shouldn't hesitate to use them. Associations like LDAQ (Learning Disabilities Association of Quebec) offer information and support services. Your local community services center (CLSC) may well offer professional services for families in your situation. While keeping in mind the resources that may exist on the local and regional level, be sure to do some hunting around; you'll no doubt find solutions to some of your problems.

A Mother's Story

"I'm going to tell you a little about my experience with my child's problem. Gabriel is a twelve-year-old boy who is in fifth grade and performs at the second or third grade level. He's in a regular class and has the help of a special educator two hours a week. Gabriel has permanent severe dyslexia and dysgraphia.

"I fought to get services for my son and to make sure teachers were informed about his learning disabilities. I spoke out on the problems my child was experiencing. I also got involved with the school board as a member of the advisory board on services for handicapped students and students with social maladjustments or learning disabilities, and served on the governing board of my school. I learned a retraining technique for children with dyslexia and used it with Gabriel; I took my son out of his English class for a year so he could concentrate more on French. I often went to the school to provide Gabriel with additional services. All this was on a volunteer basis.

"At present, I'm working in an elementary school, from kindergarten to third grade, and I've set up a multisensory program for children with learning disabilities. In the program, the children learn games, music, and relaxation techniques by using all their senses. I'm putting a lot into this project because I firmly believe that we all learn in different ways.

"Now that I've raised awareness about my son's learning disabilities at the elementary level, I have to do the same thing in secondary school. Gabriel has one more year of elementary school. It takes more effort to increase awareness in the secondary school environment, so it won't be easy. It's like starting all over; once again, I'll have to approach the teachers and other staff members who'll be working with Gabriel.

"The Learning Disabilities Association of Quebec has given me courage and support. I work with LDAQ as a volunteer, answering calls from parents who are looking for information and encouragement, and it's very gratifying work."

A mother, representative of an LDAQ committee

Remember

- The Quebec *Education Act* recognizes that parents are entitled to be involved in their children's individualized education plan.

- Parents are a permanent link between their children and the school.

- Students with learning disabilities are entitled to instructional services and special education services.

CHAPTER 8

ANSWERS TO FREQUENTLY ASKED QUESTIONS

▼

My son has failed in school repeatedly. They say he's intelligent, but lazy and unmotivated. Could he have learning disabilities?

Failure in school can be indicative of learning disabilities. Children with disabilities are often described as lazy because they can perform well in some subjects while failing in others. A thorough evaluation of the problem is necessary.

Can the family or social milieu cause learning disabilities?

Neither the family nor the social milieu causes learning disabilities. Learning disabilities are intrinsic to the child. However, similar disabilities may be found in a parent or other family member.

Who is competent to evaluate and diagnose learning disabilities?

The competent people are qualified professionals such as school psychologists, special education teachers, speech therapists, neuropsychologists, pediatricians and psychiatrists. It is highly recommended that this task be performed by a multidisciplinary team.

Should my child's difficulties be evaluated by the school?

Yes. The school board is required to evaluate students, and the school is responsible for establishing the individualized education plan (IEP). You have to find out when your child will be evaluated and when the education plan will be drawn up so that you can participate in these meetings.

What do I need to know before going to a professional in a private clinic to have my child's learning disabilities evaluated and diagnosed?

You must make sure that the professional you consult is very familiar with learning disabilities. You also need to find out whether the school will recognize the evaluation. Will the school pay for it? Is the cost covered by your insurance?

The school is advising me that my child should be taking Ritalin. What should I do?

Parents are free to accept or refuse medication for their child, even if the school recommends it. In any case, Ritalin is available only by doctor's prescription, and should be closely monitored by the prescribing physician, whether the latter is a pediatrician, psychiatrist or neurologist.

Would repeating a grade help my child learn in school?

Research indicates that having a child repeat a grade has major negative effects which can later lead to the student's dropping out of school.

The school suggests putting my child in a class for children with serious learning disabilities. Can I refuse this option?

Yes, you can refuse if you feel the services offered in this class don't meet your child's needs. First, however, you should consult the school principal and the teacher, because the option may be beneficial and the class may offer excellent special services. In any case, make sure you are adequately informed before signing your child's transfer.

What should I know about the individualized education plan? Is it mandatory when a student is socially maladjusted or has a learning disability?

Yes, the individualized education plan is obligatory for students with a social maladjustment or learning disability. The IEP specifies the services the student will receive during a given period. It must take into account the student's evaluation and particular needs. The plan requires the active participation of the parents and the school staff. The school principal is responsible for making sure the plan is implemented.

My child has learning disabilities and the school says it doesn't have the financial resources to provide services for her. Whom should I ask for help?

In such circumstances, it is your job to act as an advocate for your child and take your request to the school board, which should have the budget to provide the services. Here is what the 1999 *Education Act* has to say on the subject:

"Every school board shall ... adapt the educational services provided to handicapped students and students with social maladjustments or learning disabilities according to their needs." (Section 234)

"Every school board shall adopt, by by-law ... standards for the organization of educational services for such students with a view to facilitating their learning and social integration.

Matters prescribed in the by-law shall include

1. procedures for evaluating handicapped students and students with social maladjustments or learning disabilities

2. methods for integrating those students into regular classes or groups and into regular school activities as well as the support services required for their integration and, if need be, the weighting required to determine the maximum number of students per class or group

3. terms and conditions for grouping those students in specialized schools, classes or groups

4. methods for preparing and evaluating the individualized education plans intended for such students."
(Section 235)

Conclusion

▼

Parents have an essential role to play in the success of their learning-disabled children. In this book, we have tried to explain what these disabilities are and to provide answers to such questions as: How do these disabilities manifest themselves? How are they evaluated? How do we learn to live with them? How can we obtain services?

This book, written in the form of a practical guide, is intended both for parents who have noticed that their child is "different" and may feel worried or discouraged, and for children (of which there are many) who experience repeated failure and feel anxious or even abandoned.

* * *

The new orientation of the Quebec Department of Education policy on special education is as follows:

"To help handicapped students or students with a social maladjustment or learning difficulties to succeed in the areas of instruction, socialization and qualification. To that end, to accept that such success takes different forms, depending on the students, and providing the means to foster such success."

This orientation provides a good indication of the considerable advances made in the past few years. While the values of competition and performance have not disappeared, society in general and the educational community in particular have become much more sensitive to the needs of children with a learning disability or social maladjustment. Whether by forming associations or by acting directly in the schools, parents have been the prime advocates of this reform, which is based on recognition of the potential of each and every child.

It is essential that more educational resources be made available to parents and teachers so they are better able to do their job as educators. It is time to find methods tailored to these students' needs to ensure that they take the right path, the path that leads to success.

Children with learning disabilities have a right to be respected and successful; their parents have a right to see their children happy.

Appendices

CHECKLISTS FOR DETECTING EARLY WARNING SIGNS OF LEARNING DISABILITIES*

▼

Who are the children at risk?

This document was designed for parents and educators, and is intended to help them detect the first signs of certain developmental and learning delays in children two to five years old. Users of these checklists are advised to place a checkmark next to the signs observed, while keeping in mind the child's age, the context in which the child is being evaluated, the child's background, the age group of the people with whom the child ordinarily spends time, and the number of weeks the observation lasts.

You shouldn't wait for a child to show all the characteristics described in the checklists before asking questions or consulting a specialist. Prior to arranging for an evaluation that will lead to a diagnosis, you should try to observe whether the difficulties experienced by the child are related to visual, auditory or motor handicaps or to emotional disturbance.

These checklists are not intended to be used in making a diagnosis, but rather as an aid to understanding how a child develops.

---

* LDAQ document prepared in collaboration with the Laval chapter. Revised and adapted by the Quebec chapter in 1998.

CHECKLIST FOR DETECTING EARLY
WARNING SIGNS

OF AUDITORY DISABILITIES

❏ 1. Doesn't react to his or her name when called.

❏ 2. Has much more difficulty paying attention during tasks in which he or she is asked to listen (for example, can draw for hours on end, but can't sit still and listen to a short story).

❏ 3. Frequently asks you to repeat what you have said.

❏ 4. Has trouble remembering nursery rhymes or learning the days of the week, while other children the same age manage these fairly easily.

❏ 5. Can't distinguish between some words that sound alike.

❏ 6. Doesn't remember the most important details about a story he or she has heard.

❏ 7. Is easily distracted and has much more difficulty than other children in understanding when in noisy surroundings (for example when music is playing, there is traffic noise, or other children are talking).

❏ 8. Understands much more easily if you are close by and he or she can see your face.

❏ 9. Understands only if you help him or her with gestures or visual indicators (for example, pointing to the object you are talking about).

❑ 10. Often looks at you without answering, with a puzzled look, or gives an answer that has nothing to do with the question.

❑ 11. Does not participate as much as you would expect in verbal exchanges with other members of the group. Tends to keep apart, seems lonely.

Resource person: audiologist

CHECKLIST FOR DETECTING EARLY WARNING SIGNS OF LEARNING DISABILITIES

RELATED TO PSYCHOLOGICAL DEVELOPMENT

1. Has an activity level that can be described as:
   - ❏ hyperactive
   - ❏ sometimes very active
   - ❏ moderately active
   - ❏ less active than peers
   - ❏ inactive.

❏ 2. Doesn't seem to learn from his or her negative experiences.

❏ 3. Can't tell right from left by the age of five and a half.

❏ 4. Tires easily.

❏ 5. Is easily distracted.

❏ 6. Can't pay attention to one thing at a time.

❏ 7. Demonstrates constant or excessive agitation.

❏ 8. Disturbs the other members of the group.

❏ 9. Needs constant supervision to function adequately.

❏ 10. Has trouble understanding what is asked of him or her and following instructions properly.

❏ 11. Needs to have information repeated because he or she doesn't remember it.

❏ 12. Seems to have trouble understanding how group or family life works and what are the rules governing it.

❏ 13. Has trouble negotiating, cooperating, or coming to an understanding with other children.

❏ 14. Has difficulty adapting to the preschool environment.

Resource person: psychologist

CHECKLIST FOR DETECTING EARLY WARNING SIGNS

OF LANGUAGE DISABILITIES

❑ 1. Doesn't seem to want to communicate with other children or adults and has difficulty establishing a relationship with others.

❑ 2. Consistently seems not to understand simple requests or questions (for example, who, what, where, what is being done) and depends on other children's actions to interpret them.

❑ 3. Expresses himself or herself mainly by looks, gestures or sounds rather than words.

❑ 4. Has trouble verbally expressing what he or she wants, making requests, giving orders, making comments and asking questions.

❑ 5. By the age of five, cannot report an event in the order in which it happened.

❑ 6. Has an immature, limited vocabulary in comparison with his or her peers, and has trouble finding the words to express his or her thoughts, even if the words are already familiar.

❑ 7. Can't say any words at 15 months, doesn't form two-word sentences at the age of two, doesn't form simple sentences (at least three or four words) at the age of three, has trouble speaking grammatically and cannot construct a correct sentence at about four or five years of age (for example, doesn't use "little" words like articles, prepositions or pronouns or doesn't conjugate verbs, e.g. "Kevin eat cake").

❏ 8. Can't pronounce words distinctly at about two-and-a half or three years of age and is still incomprehensible at about four.

❏ 9. Still distorts words and sentences to some extent at the age of five.

Resource person: speech therapist

CHECKLIST FOR DETECTING EARLY WARNING SIGNS

OF READING AND WRITING DISABILITIES (4-5 YEARS OLD)

N.B. This checklist applies specifically to children of preschool age (4-5) and is more concerned with learning than development.

- [ ] 1. Is unaware of the act of reading.

- [ ] 2. Has not developed basic reading skills (for example, following with his or her finger from left to right or from top to bottom).

- [ ] 3. Doesn't recognize the title of a book already read.

- [ ] 4. Can't find a page in a book.

- [ ] 5. Doesn't recognize familiar letters alone on a page.

- 6. Doesn't understand the following:
  - [ ] middle of the page
  - [ ] bottom of the page
  - [ ] top of the page.

- [ ] 7. Can't recognize at least four advertising signs or logos in his or her surroundings.

- [ ] 8. Can't tell the first names of two nursery school classmates.

- [ ] 9. Can't identify at least two lower-case letters.

- [ ] 10. Can't identify at least three upper-case letters.

❏ 11. Can't identify or doesn't seem to understand the following terms of comparison: less than, more than, same amount (like).

Resource person: special education teacher

CHECKLIST FOR DETECTING EARLY WARNING SIGNS

OF MOTOR AND COORDINATION DISABILITIES

❏ 1. Tends not to know his or her own strength (presses too hard on the pencil, hugs friends too tightly).

❏ 2. Demonstrates hypotonicity: is always leaning on something, is unable to form a bridge or wheelbarrow with his or her body, imitate an airplane, etc.

❏ 3. Is afraid of heights or of trying out slides or seesaws.

❏ 4. Seems clumsy (lacking in motor dexterity): is "all thumbs" or drops things often; trips over his or her own feet, bumps into things.

❏ 5. Shows minimum interest in board games or tends to avoid them.

❏ 6. Grasps a pencil clumsily. Has trouble using scissors.

❏ 7. Has a hard time reproducing lines or simple geometric shapes.

❏ 8. Draws like someone very immature or is still at the scribbling stage.

❏ 9. Is slow in doing things, lacks organization, doesn't know how to do a given task.

❏ 10. Avoids physical contact: uncomfortable with certain textures (e.g. glue, paint, fur), tends to wear clothes that completely cover the body and prefers non-restrictive clothes.

Resource person: occupational therapist

CHECKLIST FOR DETECTING EARLY WARNING SIGNS

OF VISUAL DISABILITIES

❏ 1. Reads and writes with eyes close to the page, holds objects close to eyes when looking at them.

❏ 2. Eyes are red and tearing after an activity requiring concentration.

❏ 3. Squints when looking into the distance and sits very close to the set when watching TV.

❏ 4. Blinks often, eyes burn or sting.

❏ 5. Closes one eye to see better or complains of double vision.

❏ 6. Is clumsy at cutting, colouring and doing craft activities.

❏ 7. Is poor at sports and games.

❏ 8. Has trouble with visual-spatial organization.

❏ 9. When reading, skips words or lines or loses the place.

❏ 10. When reading and writing, reverses letters, syllables and words.

Resource person: optometrist

Extract from:
STUDENTS WITH HANDICAPS, SOCIAL MALADJUSTMENTS OR LEARNING DIFFICULTIES: DEFINITIONS*

▼

Students with social maladjustments or learning difficulties

At-Risk Students

At-risk students are students who require special support measures because they:

- experience difficulties that may lead to failure;
- exhibit learning delays;
- have emotional disorders;
- have behavioural disorders;
- have a developmental delay or a mild intellectual impairment.

---

* Ministère de l'Éducation du Québec (2000 — 00-0237)

By way of example, at-risk children or students may exhibit some of the following characteristics:

Preschool:

- have frequent discipline problems,
- are isolated, do not mix with other students,
- have an expressive language delay (without a language disorder),
- experience difficulty in following instructions given by an adult,
- experience difficulty in selecting, processing, retaining and using information,
- manifest a delay in awareness of written language and numbers,
- have attention deficits,
- have a developmental delay,
- have behavioural disorders.

Elementary:

- experience difficulty attaining the objectives of the Québec Education Program,
- have an expressive language delay (without a language disorder),
- are considered overrreactive (discipline problems, attention deficit) or underactive (minimal interaction with classmates),
- have learning difficulties or disorders,
- have a mild intellectual impairment,
- have emotional problems,
- have behavioural disorders.

Secondary:

- have an academic delay,
- have learning difficulties or disorders,
- have a mild intellectual impairment,
- have non-academic difficulties (pregnancy, anorexia, depression, addiction, etc.),
- have emotional problems,
- have missed several classes, without a valid reason,
- have been involved in several incidents related to discipline (suspension, detention, etc.),
- have behavioural disorders.

Other students experience difficulties because they are not proficient in the language of instruction, are not adapted to the host culture, or do not understand the subtleties of the language, despite measures such as welcoming classes or despite having spent time in an ordinary classroom. They too may need special services.

Resources

▼

Organizations and Agencies

The education community: school, school board, Department of Education (especially the Special Education Bureau)

The healthcare community: family doctor, pediatrician, learning clinics in hospitals, local community services centers, etc.

National and Regional Community Organizations and Agencies

Quebec

Human Rights Commission
Tel.: (514) 873-5146

Learning Disabilities Association of Quebec (LDAQ)
Tel.: (514) 847-1324

Canada

Learning Disabilities Association of Canada (LDAC)
Tel.: (613) 238-5721

Learning Disabilities Association of British Columbia
Tel.: (604) 873-8139

Learning Disabilities Association of Alberta
Tel.: (403) 438-0665

Learning Disabilities Association of Saskatchewan
Tel.: (306) 652-4114

Learning Disabilities Association of Manitoba
Tel.: (204) 774-1821

Learning Disabilities Association of Ontario
Tel.: (416) 929-4311

Learning Disabilities Association of New Brunswick
Tel.: (506) 459-7852

Learning Disabilities Association of Nova Scotia
Tel.: (902) 464-9751

Learning Disabilities Association of Prince Edward Island
Tel.: (902) 892-9664

Learning Disabilities Association of Newfoundland
Tel.: (709) 754-3665

USA

Children and Adults with Attention Deficit Disorder (CHADD)
Tel.: (954) 587-3700

International Dyslexia Association (formerly the Orton Dyslexia Association)
Tel.: 1 (800) 222-3123

Learning Disabilities Association of America (LDAA)
Tel.: (412) 341-1515

Books and Brochures

BARKLEY, RUSSEL A. *Taking Charge of ADHD*. New York: The Guilford Press. 1995.

CLARK, LYNN. *SOS? Help for Parents*. Bowling Green, Kentucky: Parents Press. 1996.

HALLOWELL, EDWARD M., M.D., AND JOHN. J. RATEY. *Answers to Distractions*. Toronto: Bantam Books. 1994.

HALLOWELL, EDWARD M., M.D., AND JOHN. J. RATEY. *Driven to Distraction*. New York: Pantheon Books. 1994.

LEARNING DISABILITIES ASSOCIATION OF CANADA. *A Guide to Understanding Learning and Behaviour Problems in Children: For Parents and Others*. Ottawa: LDAC, 1996.

LEARNING DISABILITIES ASSOCIATION OF CANADA. *Advocating for Your Child with Learning Disabilities*. Ottawa: LDAC, 1998.

DROVER, JANE, LYNN OWEN AND ALEXANDER WILSON. *A Family Affair: Preparing Parents and Students with Learning Disabilities for Postsecondary Education*. Ottawa: LDAC, 1998.

Web Sites

Children and Adults with Attention Deficit Disorder (CHADD)
www.chadd.org

Child & Family Canada
www.cfc-efc.ca

> The Canadian Association of Family Resource Programs provides articles of interest to parents of children with learning disabilities, including the following:

> JEAN A. NESS. "The High Jump: Transition Issues of Learning Disabled Students and their Parents"
> www.cfc-efc.ca/docs/00000357.htm

> JULIE A. DINSMORE AND DOUGLAS ISAACSON. "Tactics for Teaching Dyslexic Students"
> www.cfc-efc.ca/docs/00000455.htm

International Dyslexia Association (IDA)
www.interdys.org

Learning Disabilities Association of America (LDAA)
www.ldanatl.org

Learning Disabilities Association of Canada (LDAC)
www.ldac-tacc.ca

Learning Disabilities Association of Quebec (LDAQ)
www.aqeta.qc.ca

AGMV Marquis

MEMBER OF THE SCABRINI GROUP

Quebec, Canada
2001

BIBLIOGRAPHY

▼

American Psychiatric Association. *DSM-IV (Diagnostic and Statistical Manual of Mental Disorders, Fourth Edition)*. Washington: American Psychiatric Association, 1994.

Direction de la coordination des réseaux, Ministère de l'Éducation du Québec. "Definitions: Students with Handicaps or Learning or Adjustment Difficulties." December 11, 1992.

Learning Disabilities Association of Canada (LDAC). *Advocating for Your Child with Learning Disabilities*. Ottawa: LDAC, 1998.

Learning Disabilities Association of Canada (LDAC). *A Guide to Understanding Learning and Behaviour Problems in Children: For Parents and Others*. Ottawa: LDAC, 1996.

Learning Disabilities Association of Quebec (LDAQ). *Obtaining services at school*. Montréal: LDAQ, 1998.

RESNICK, I.J., D.A. ALLAN, I. RAPIN. "Disorders of Language Development: Diagnosis and Intervention." *Pediatrics in Review*, Vol. 6, No. 3, September 1984.

SILVER, LARRY B. *Attention-Deficit Hyperactivity Disorder and Learning Disabilities*. A Booklet for Parents. American Psychiatric Press, 1992.